Q AND A

The little book of questions on.....

CARAMELS

Copyright © 2013 Two Magpies Publishing
An imprint of Read Publishing Ltd
Home Farm, 44 Evesham Road, Cookhill, Alcester,
Warwickshire, B49 5LJ

Commissioning Editor Rose Hewlett
Words by Sophie Berry
Design and Illustrations by Zoë Horn Haywood

British Library Cataloguing-in-Publication Data A catalogue
record for this book is available from the British Library.

CONTENTS

INTRODUCTION

MAKE LOVINGLY CREATED CONFECTIONERY!

Making caramels is a fascinating craft. Watching the changing appearance and behaviour of a batch of sugar at various temperatures turns a novice cook into an eager scientist, with a thirst for experiment.

As a pastime it can be guaranteed never to lose its thrill, from the first burnt saucepan of a beginner, to the perfectly formed caramels of the experienced creator.

The beauty of making your own caramels is that you can be sure to use the best and purest ingredients. In an age which tends to be increasingly synthetic, knowing exactly what has gone into your lovingly created confectionery is an attractive prospect.

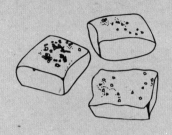

Added to this, the result of making caramels at home is often much cheaper than buying them ready-made. By only making what you want, and in quantities you need, there is no waste.

Hopefully you are now feeling inspired to get your first batch on the stove. This little book will endeavour to answer any questions you have about the caramel-making process, from which pan is best to use, to how to tell when your creation is ready.

ALL THAT'S LEFT TO SAY IS -
GOOD LUCK!

HISTORY

Q. Where did the word 'caramel' come from?

A. The origin of the word has been traced to the Medieval Latin word cannamellis, which means sugar cane.

Q. What is the difference between caramel, and caramels?

A. Caramel is a thin, sauce-type substance which is used as an accompaniment to desserts. Caramels are soft, chewy sweets.

Q. Are there different types of caramels?

A. Yes, there are a two different types of caramels. the main difference is the use, or absence of cream. Cream caramels are, as their name suggests, creamy and lighter in colour than caramels made without cream.

Q. Where were caramels first made?

A. Many people believe caramels originated from America, where they have been made since the seventeenth century.

Q. What about cream caramels?

A. In the mid-1800s, curious cooks realised that by adding milk and butter to their caramels as the mixture cooked, a sweeter, creamier confection could be produced.

Q. Are caramels still popular?

A. Today, caramels, and caramel are still very popular all over the world. Caramel is found as an ingredient in a host of commercial chocolate bars, like Mars bars, and Cadbury's Caramel. Caramel sauce is also extremely popular, and found in many desserts, and ice cream.

EQUIPMENT

Q. Will I need lots of specialist equipment?

A. No. Equipment is simple. You'll need a heavy-bottomed pan, preferably a copper-bottom jam boiler. A smaller, heavy-bottomed pan will also be useful, as some of the recipes in this book will call for you to use two saucepans.

Q. How big should the pan be that I use?

A. Your largest pan should be big enough to hold twice the bulk you are likely to need, as boiling sugar bubbles expand a lot.

Q. Will I need a thermometer?

A. Yes, a thermometer is essential. A sugar-boiling thermometer with the various stages marked will be very useful.

Q. What about utensils?

A. You'll need a wooden spoon for stirring, a large bowl, a set of scales, and a sieve, or colander.

Q. Will I need to use molds to shape my caramels?

A. No, you can pour your mixture into a shallow baking tin to cool.

Q. How do I make sure the caramels don't stick to the pan?

A. Ensure you line your baking tin with baking paper, or grease the tin with vegetable oil or butter. You can use both of these methods to ensure your sweets do not stick to the pan.

Q. How do I make my caramels into bite-sized sweets?

A. Make sure you mark your caramels mixture into little squares with a sharp knife before it cools completely. You can then snap along the marks you made, and break into bite-sized sweets.

COOKING SUGAR

PREPARATION

Q. Most of the recipes I have seen use cups as a measurement. How much is a cup?

A. You will see that cups are used as measurements in many recipes. A small coffee cup is the best kind to use, and make sure you use the same cup to measure all your ingredients.

Of course, you don't have to use cups. This table is a handy tool if you need to convert cups into other amounts.

CUP MEASURMENTS

1 cup	8 fluid ounces	½ pint	237 ml
2 cups	16 fluid ounces	1 pint	474 ml
4 cups	32 fluid ounces	1 quart	946 ml
2 pints	32 fluid ounces	1 quart	0.946 l
4 quarts	128 fluid ounces	1 gallon	3.784 l

Q. What is the best way to test the temperature as I heat the mixture?

A. A thermometer is the best way to accurately test the temperature of your caramels mixture as it cooks.

Q. Can I tell if my mixture is cooked without using a thermometer?

A. If you don't have a thermometer, you can determine the temperature of your mixture with the Drop Test, which is when you drop a little mixture into cold water.

Q. What should the mixture look like when its dropped into cold water?

A. Most of the recipes in this book will state to heat the mixture to firm ball stage, which is around 240 to 250°F. If you drop a little mixture into some cold water and the liquid forms a firm ball, then you have reached the temperature required to make caramels.

Have a look at the Drop Test table here for more information on monitoring the temperature of your caramels mixture without a thermometer.

SUGAR STAGES

STAGE when the mixture is tested in cold water	TEMPERATURE	USES
THREAD Forms a thin liquid thread	110 to 112 °C (230 to 234 °F)	Sugar Syrups
SOFT BALL Forms a soft flexible ball that can be flattened	112 to 116 °C (234 to 241 °F)	Fudge, pralines, fondant and butter creams
FIRM BALL Forms a firm ball that will hold its shape but is still malleable	118 to 120 °C (244 to 248 °F)	Caramel Candies
HARD BALL Forms thick threads from spoon and creates a hard ball that will hold its shape	121 to 130 °C (250 to 266 °F)	Nougat, marshmallows, gummies, and divinity
SOFT CRACK Forms firm flexible threads	132 to 143 °C (270 to 289 °F)	salt water taffy
HARD CRACK Forms hard brittle threads that snap easily	146 to 154 °C (295 to 309 °F)	toffee, brittles, hard candy, and lollipops
CLEAR LIQUID Liquid will begin to change colour. Colour ranges from golden brown to amber	160 °C (320 °F)	caramelised sugar, caramel
BROWN LIQUID Liquid will begin to change colour. Colour ranges from golden brown to amber	170 °C (338 °F)	caramelised sugar, caramel

RECIPES

Q. What is a good traditional caramels recipe to start with?

A. The distinctive flavour of vanilla is a key ingredient in lots of classic recipes for caramels. Try this simple recipe for traditional vanilla caramels.

VANILLA CARAMELS

INGREDIENTS

1 lb sugar
4 oz glucose
2 oz butter
½ cup condensed milk
½ cup water
¼ tsp vanilla essence

METHOD

1. In a heavy-bottomed saucepan, heat the sugar, glucose and water to 250°F, or until the mixture forms a firm ball when tested in cold water.

2. Remove the pan from the heat, and add the milk and butter. Stir well.

3. Add the vanilla essence, return the pan to the heat and stir well until the mixture is boiling.

4. Carefully pour the mixture into an oiled baking tin, and mark into squares when cool.

Q. What other flavours can you add to caramels?

A. Peppermint works wonderfully as an additional flavour in caramels. Adding peppermint to your sweets makes them a perfect after-dinner offering.

PEPPERMINT CARAMELS

INGREDIENTS

1 lb sugar
4 oz glucose
2 oz butter
½ cup condensed milk
½ cup water
¼ tsp peppermint oil

METHOD

1. In a heavy-bottomed saucepan, heat the sugar, glucose and water to 250°F, or until the mixture forms a firm ball when tested in cold water.

2. Remove the pan from the heat, and add the milk and butter. Stir well.

3. Add the peppermint oil, return the pan to the heat and stir well until the the mixture is boiling.

4. Carefully pour the mixture into an oiled baking tin, and mark into squares when cool.

Q. Is it possible to add fruit flavours to caramels?

A. Yes. Fruity caramels are a real treat, and adding fruit to your sweets will give them a lovely pop of colour. This recipe for raspberry caramels rather ingeniously uses jam, and a little red food colouring to make for a distinctive sweet. Why not get creative, and try substituting raspberry jam for another fruit conserve?

RASPBERRY CARAMELS

INGREDIENTS

1 lb sugar
4 oz glucose.
2 oz butter, cubed
¼ tsp red food colouring
4 oz raspberry jam
½ cup condensed milk
½ cup water

METHOD

1. In a heavy-bottomed saucepan, heat the sugar, glucose and water to 250°F, or until the mixture forms a firm ball when tested in cold water.

2. Remove the pan from the heat, and add the milk, butter and jam. Stir well,

3. Add the colouring, return the pan to the heat and stir well until the the mixture is boiling.

4. Carefully pour the mixture into an oiled baking tin, and mark into squares when cool.

Q. Can you use citrus fruits when making caramels?

A. Yes, the zest of citrus fruit is a fabulous addition to your homemade caramels, and adds a hint of colour as well as a great, zingy taste to your sweets. You can use the zest of any fruit you wish, but a mixture of zest will create a brilliantly bright batch of caramels.

ZESTY CARAMELS

INGREDIENTS

1 lb sugar
4 oz glucose
2 oz butter
½ cup condensed milk
½ cup water
¼ tsp lemon essence
1 tbsp citrus zest
(you can use a mixture of fruit zest if you like)

METHOD

1. In a heavy-bottomed saucepan, heat the sugar, glucose and water to 250°F, or until the mixture forms a firm ball when tested in cold water.

2. Remove the pan from the heat, and add the milk and butter. Stir well.

3. Add the vanilla essence, return the pan to the heat and stir well until the the mixture is boiling.

4. Carefully pour the mixture into an oiled baking tin, and sprinkle over the citrus zest.

5. Mark into squares when cool.

Q. Can you add dried fruit to caramels?

A. Fruit works brilliantly alongside the sweet taste of caramels. This recipe for fruit caramels uses figs, but you can use any dried fruit you like. Raisins, cherries, and cranberries also work really well.

FIG CARAMELS

INGREDIENTS

1 lb sugar
4 oz glucose
2 oz butter
½ cup condensed milk
½ cup water
¼ tsp orange essence
4 figs, chopped

METHOD

1. In a heavy-bottomed saucepan, heat the sugar, glucose and water to 250°F, or until the mixture forms a firm ball when tested in cold water.

2. Remove the pan from the heat, and add the milk and butter. Stir well.

3. Add the figs and essence, return the pan to the heat and stir well until the the mixture is boiling.

4. Carefully pour the mixture into an oiled baking tin, and mark into squares when cool.

Q. Do you have to use granulated sugar when making caramels, or can you use other types?

A. Most recipes simply call for regular granulated sugar, but you will also find more unusual ingredients in some recipes such as this one which uses maple sugar.

MAPLE CARAMELS

INGREDIENTS

⅔ cup maple sugar
⅔ cup white sugar
½ cup corn syrup
2 cups single cream

METHOD

1. In a heavy-bottomed saucepan, heat the sugar, corn syrup, and half a cup of the cream over a low heat. Stir until the sugar has dissolved.

2. Bring the mixture to the boil, and heat until to 240°F, or until the mixture forms a soft ball when tested in cold water.

3. Add another half cup of cream, stirring constantly.

4. Bring the mixture back to the boil, and when the mixture again reaches 240°F, or forms a soft ball when tested in cold water, add the remaining cream.

5. Heat the mixture to 250°F, or until the mixture forms a firm ball when tested in cold water.

6. Carefully pour the mixture into an oiled baking tin, and mark into squares when cool.

Q. Is it possible to make caramels with honey? I'd like to try a recipe which uses less sugar than the classic recipes for caramels.

A. Yes, you can use honey to make caramels. Try this simple recipe for honey caramels.

HONEY CARAMELS

INGREDIENTS

½ cup honey
¼ cup single cream
½ cup Demerara sugar
1 tsp vanilla essence
1 tbsp glucose
1 oz butter

METHOD

1. In a heavy-bottomed saucepan, combine the honey, single cream, sugar, glucose and butter and stir over a low heat.

2. When the sugar has dissolved, bring the mixture to the boil.

3. Heat the mixture until it reaches 250°F, or until the mixture forms a hard ball when tested in cold water.

4. Remove the pan from the heat and add the vanilla essence. Stir well.

5. Carefully pour the mixture into an oiled baking tin and mark into squares when cool.

Q.

Can you add nuts to caramels?

A.

Yes, nuts are a wonderful addition to caramels. When using nuts in your recipe, make sure they are unsalted, and chopped coarsely. Chopping the nuts too finely will make the sweets take on an almost 'gritty' texture. A very quick blitz in a food processor is a quick and easy way to prepare your nut meats.

WALNUT CARAMELS

INGREDIENTS

1 lbs sugar
½ cup shelled walnuts, chopped
4 oz glucose
2 oz butter, cubed
¼ tsp saffron food colouring
½ cup condensed milk
½ cup water

METHOD

1. In a heavy-bottomed saucepan, heat the sugar, glucose and water to 250°F, or until the mixture forms a firm ball when tested in cold water.

2. Remove the pan from the heat, and add the milk and butter. Stir well.

3. Add the walnuts and essence, return the pan to the heat and stir well until the the mixture is boiling.

4. Carefully pour the mixture into an oiled baking tin, and mark into squares when cool.

Q. Can you add chocolate to caramels?

A. Yes, chocolate is a popular addition to caramels, and you will find that many classic recipes include chocolate. Try this simple recipe for chocolate almond caramels.

CHOCOLATE ALMOND CARAMELS

INGREDIENTS

1 lb sugar
¼ lb glucose
2 oz butter
½ cup condensed milk
½ cup water
¼ tsp vanilla essence
½ cup almonds, chopped
2 squares chocolate, grated

METHOD

1. In a heavy-bottomed saucepan heat the sugar, glucose and water to 250°F, or until the mixture forms a firm ball when tested in cold water.

2. Remove the pan from the heat, and add the milk and butter. Stir well.

3. Add the grated chocolate, vanilla essence and chopped almonds, return the pan to the heat and stir well until the the mixture is boiling.

4. Carefully pour the mixture into an oiled baking tin, and mark into squares when cool.

Q. Can you add alcohol to caramel?

A. Yes! Kahlúa, the coffee-based liqueur works perfectly with the sweetness of caramels. Try this recipe for Kahlúa coffee caramels, which make a fantastic grown-up treat.

KAHLÚA COFFEE CARAMELS

INGREDIENTS

2 cups sugar
¼ cups golden syrup
1 cup double cream
¼ cups butter
½ tsp salt
2 tbsp coffee
2 tbsp Khalúa

METHOD

1. In a heavy-bottomed saucepan, combine all the ingredients.

2. Stir over a low heat until the sugar has dissolved.

3. Heat the mixture until it reaches 250°F, or until the mixture forms a firm ball when tested in cold water.

4. Carefully pour the mixture into a lightly buttered baking tin.

5. Mark into squares when cool.

Q.

Is there a simple coffee caramel recipe I can try which doesn't use liqueur?

A.

Yes, this liqueur-free coffee caramels recipe is really straightforward.

COFFEE CARAMELS

INGREDIENTS

1 lb sugar
4 oz glucose
2 oz butter
½ cup condensed milk
½ cup water
¼ cup strong coffee

METHOD

1. In a heavy-bottomed saucepan, heat the sugar, glucose and water to 250°F, or until the mixture forms a firm ball when tested in cold water.

2. Remove the pan from the heat, and add the milk and butter. Stir well.

3. Add the coffee to the mixture, and return the pan to the heat. Stir well until the the mixture is boiling.

4. Carefully pour the mixture into an oiled baking tin, and mark into squares when cool.

Q. Are there any recipes for caramels which include coconut?

A. Yes, coconut is a fantastic addition to caramels as the distinctive flavour complements the sweetness perfectly. Granulated coconut is readily available, and very easy to use in your recipes as all the preparation has been done for you! Try this simple recipe for wonderfully creamy coconut caramels.

COCONUT CARAMELS

INGREDIENTS

1 lb sugar
4 oz glucose
2 oz butter, cubed
2 oz granulated or dessicated coconut, unsweetened
½ cup condensed milk
½ cup water

METHOD

1. In a heavy-bottomed saucepan, heat the sugar, glucose and water to 250°F, or until the mixture forms a firm ball when tested in cold water.

2. Remove the pan from the heat, and add the milk and butter. Stir well.

3. Add the coconut, return the pan to the heat and stir well until the the mixture is boiling.

4. Carefully pour the mixture into an oiled baking tin, and mark into squares when cool.

Q. What other fun ingredients can I add to my caramels? I'd love to try something really unusual!

A. Caramels are a brilliantly versatile confectionery, and you can even add herbs to your sweets giving them a complex taste and lovely aroma. Try this unusual recipe for rosemary caramels, which uses a sprig of the popular garden herb to infuse the mixture with its unmistakable flavour.

ROSEMARY CARAMELS

INGREDIENTS

1 sprig fresh rosemary
1 ½ cups double cream
4 oz butter
1 cup light corn syrup
2 cups sugar

1 tsp salt
1 tsp vanilla extract
1 tsp orange zest
½ cup toasted, salted pistachios

METHOD

1. In a heavy-bottomed saucepan, heat the rosemary, cream, and half of the butter over a medium heat. Bring the mixture to a low boil.

2. Remove the pan from the heat and leave the mixture for 45 minutes to infuse the flavours.

3. Combine the corn syrup and the sugar in a small saucepan and place the pan over medium to high heat. Stir until the sugar dissolves and the mixture comes to a boil. Heat until the mixture reaches 320°F, or until the mixture remains a clear liquid when tested in cold water.

4. Remove the sugar and syrup pan from the heat. Return to the pan containing the cream, butter and rosemary, and carefully pour the mixture through a strainer into the hot sugar syrup, straining out the rosemary sprig. Be careful not to splash yourself with the hot syrup.

5. Return the pan containing the now-combined ingredients to the heat. Cook the caramel, stirring frequently, until the mixture reaches 250°F, or until the mixture forms a hard ball when tested in cold water.

6. Remove the pan from the heat and stir in the remaining 2 ounces of butter, the salt, the vanilla extract, and the orange zest.

7. Stir in the pistachios. Carefully pour the caramel into a lightly buttered baking tin and mark into squares once cool.

Q. What kind of cream do you have to use when making cream caramels?

A. Different recipes call for different types of cream, and both single and double cream are used in this book. You could also try using Jersey cream, the extra-thick cream made from the rich milk Jersey cows produce. Jersey cream caramels are particularly distinctive, as they consist of white caramel, sandwiched between a layer of cream caramel.

JERSEY CREAM CARAMELS

INGREDIENTS

For the cream caramel:
2 cups white sugar
1 ½ cups corn syrup
2 cups Jersey cream
1 cup butter
1 tsp vanilla essence

For the white caramel:
1 cup white sugar
¾ cup corn syrup
1 cup jersey cream
1 cup butter
6 squares white chocolate, chopped

METHOD

1. In a heavy-bottomed saucepan, combine two cups of white sugar, one-and-a-half cups of corn syrup, one cup of butter and one cup of Jersey cream. Bring to a boil, stirring often.

2. Stir in another cup of Jersey cream and heat the mixture to 242° F, or until the mixture forms a soft ball when tested in cold water.

3. Remove the pan from the heat and stir in the vanilla essence.

4. Carefully pour half of the mixture into a lightly buttered baking tin, and return the pan to the stove, over a very low heat.

5. In another heavy-bottomed saucepan, combine one cup of white sugar, three quarters of a cup of corn syrup, one cup of butter and half a cup of Jersey cream. Bring to a boil, stirring often.

6. Drop in the white chocolate and stir until it is melted. Add the remaining Jersey cream, and heat the mixture to 242° F, or until the mixture forms a soft ball when tested in cold water.

7. Carefully pour the white caramel mixture over the first batch of caramel mixture. Leave to cool slightly.

8. Pour the remaining caramel mixture over the white caramel. Cut into squares when cool.

Q.

Can you add marshmallows to caramels?

A.

Marshmallows are a fun addition to your caramels, and will give your sweets a slightly light and fluffy texture. This recipe uses large marshmallows, cut into quarters, but you can use multi-coloured mini marshmallows for a sweet treat that children will love.

MARSHMALLOW CARAMELS

INGREDIENTS

1 lb sugar
4 oz glucose
2 oz butter
½ cup condensed milk
½ cup water
¼ tsp cinnamon syrup
8 large marshmallows, chopped into quarters

METHOD

1. In a heavy-bottomed saucepan, heat the sugar, glucose and water to 250°F, or until the mixture forms a firm ball when tested in cold water.

2. Remove the pan from the heat, and add the milk and butter. Stir well.

3. Add the essence, return the pan to the heat and stir well until the the mixture is boiling.

4. Remove from the heat, and add the marshmallows. Stir well.

5. Carefully pour the mixture into an oiled baking tin, and mark into squares when cool.

Q. Is there a simple recipe for caramels that children can help make?

A. This ingenious recipe for caramels uses a microwave to heat the ingredients, which is a little bit more child-friendly than the traditional method of heating the sugar on the stove.

MICROWAVE CARAMEL

INGREDIENTS

¼ cup butter, cubed
½ cup white sugar
½ cup brown sugar
½ cup light corn syrup
½ cup evaporated milk

METHOD

1. In a large microwave-safe bowl stir together the butter, white and brown sugar, corn syrup, and evaporated milk.

2. Cook in a microwave on full power for 6 minutes, stopping and stirring thoroughly twice every two minutes.

3. Remove the bowl from microwave and stir until the mixture is thoroughly blended.

4. Carefully pour the mixture into a baking tin lined with baking paper.

5. Mark into squares when cool.

1. Buy a thermometer – It will make your caramel-making a lot simpler, and much more accurate

2. Make sure you 'break in' a new thermometer. Put the thermometer into a pan of cold water, bring the pan to the boil, and leave it there until the water has cooled.

3. After using your thermometer to test the temperature, plunge it into warm water and wipe it straight away.

4. Have all your ingredients measured and ready before you begin. Making caramels needs much precision, and having everything ready will ensure nothing is overcooked.

5. Follow the recipe exactly. Until you have a lot of experience making caramels, it is best to follow recipes exactly. When you become more confident, you can experiment with your own variations.

6. Make sure you remember to grease your baking tin well with vegetable oil or butter before pouring the mixture in to cool.

7. If you are worried about the mixture sticking to the pan, line it with baking paper and grease the baking paper, too.

8. Once you have poured the mixture out of the pan, immediately fill the pan with hot water and return it to the heat for a few minutes. This will stop your mixture setting onto the pan and will make it a lot easier to clean.

9. Wrapping your caramels individually in either cellophane or baking paper will stop them sticking together while they are being stored.

10. It is best to store your caramels somewhere cool.

NOTES

NOTES

Image Credits

All Pages - This work is a derivative of "Textures Paper IMG_0006" is Copyright ©2007-2012 ~Dioma, made available on DeviantArt under Creative Commons Attribution 2.0 Generic (CC BY 2.0) http//dioma.deviantart.com/art/Textures-Paper-58028330

All Pages - This work is a derivative of "Textures Paper IMG_0002" is Copyright ©2007-2012 Dioma, made available on DeviantArt under Creative Commons Attribution 2.0 Generic (CC BY 2.0) http//dioma.deviantart.com/art/Textures-Paper-58028330

All Chapter Pages - This work is a derivative of "Frame back" is copyright © 2009 Sunset Sailor made available on Flickr under Creative Commons Attribution 2.0 Generic (CC BY 2.0) http//www.flickr.com/photos/sunsetsailor/3558408492

Pages 2-3 This work is a derivative of "Mar:3" is copyright © 2011 Kim Love, lovlihood available on Flickr under Creative Commons Attribution 2.0 Generic (CC BY 2.0) http://www.flickr.com/photos/lovelihood/5496435120/in/faves-90808113@N04/

Pages 6-7 This work is a derivative of "Chocolate Caramel Cookies with Sea Salt - Caramel balls" is copyright © 2012 Rebecca Siegel, Grongar, available on Flickr under Creative Commons Attribution 2.0 Generic (CC BY 2.0) http://www.flickr.com/photos/grongar/8275184723/sizes/o/in/faves-90808113@N04/

Pages 14-15 - This work is a derivative of "Pots and Pans" is copyright © 2012 jeeheon made available on Flickr under Creative Commons Attribution 2.0 Generic (CC BY 2.0) http//www.flickr.com/photos/jeeheon/7877017204

Page 23 - This work is a derivative of "Project 365 #169: 180611 Fire Burn And Cauldron Bubble..." is copyright © 2011 comedy_nose, made available on Flickr under Creative Commons Attribution 2.0 Generic (CC BY 2.0) http://www.flickr.com/photos/comedynose/5845889514/

Pages 24-52 - This work is a derivative of "Kitchen Tools at the Table" is copyright © 2012, slightly everything, Kate Hiscock, made available on Flickr under Creative Commons Attribution 2.0 Generic (CC BY 2.0) http//www.flickr.com/photos/slightlyeverything/8229722025

Pages 32-33 This work is a derivative of "Caramels" is copyright © 2010 Kate Hopkins, Accidental Hedonist, available on Flickr under Creative Commons Attribution 2.0 Generic (CC BY 2.0) http://www.flickr.com/photos/accidentalhedonist/4786075725/